Restored By Grace

Words To Motivate And Encourage

by

M. Ann Billiet

© 2004 M. Ann Billiet.
P.O. Box 1501
Troy, Michigan 48099-1501
All rights reserved.

No part of this book may be reproduced, stored in a retrieval system, or transmitted by any means, electronic, mechanical, photocopying, recording, or otherwise, without written permission from the author.

Biblical References:

All Scripture quotations, unless otherwise indicated, are taken from the QuickVerse. 4.0 Bible Reference Collection, New International Version. Copyright 1996 by Parsons Technology, Inc. Used by permission. All rights reserved. Scripture quotations, marked KJV, are taken from the King James Version of the Bible from the QuickVerse 4.0 Bible Reference Collection. Used by permission.

ISBN: 1-4140-4997-8 (electronic)
ISBN: 1-4140-4998-6 (softcover)

Library of Congress Control Number: 2003099351

This book is printed on acid free paper.

Printed in the United States of America
Bloomington, IN

1stBooks – rev.12/26/03

God's grace is available to all of his people. All we have to do is believe and appropriate His grace in our lives. This book is about my personal life and testimony of how God's wonderful grace has restored my life, and also some thoughts on what I have learned from walking with the Lord for 30 years.

My prayer is that Gods people who read this will be encouraged and strengthened to go all the way with God and to finish the race strong so God can say to you, "Well done, thou good and faithful servant". (NIV Matthew 25:21 - "His master replied, 'Well done, good and faithful servant! You have been faithful with a few things; I will put you in charge of many things. Come and share your master's happiness!')

Also my prayer is that anyone who reads this book and does not have a personal relationship with the Lord, will pray the prayer of salvation. May God bless everyone who reads this book.

M. Ann Billiet

Acknowledgements

First, my thanks and praise and all glory for this book goes to God.

Second, for my husband, Jerry, who not only loves me, but has been my best friend. Thanks from the bottom of my heart for all of your help in making this book a reality. Without your help and support, I could not have done it.

Third, my thanks goes to the many people who have prayed for me to write and finish this book. May God bless you abundantly from his rich grace and mercy.

Also, thanks to my four daughters: Renee, Susan, Kim, and Kay, who have supported and encouraged me, and my grandchildren; Amanda, Ashley, Amber, Nicole, and Cassie.

Table of Contents

Where to Begin 1
Rainbows 3
The Beginning 5
Grandmothers 7
What next? 9
Compassion 11
Is Life Easy? No! 13
Some Experiences 19
Wellspring Ministry 27
Unity 29
The Vine - Jesus 33
You, Again? 37
Joy 47
A Word To The Unsaved 51
Pride-Who Me? 55
Mirrors 57
Memories 65
Encouragement 71
Spiritual Leaders 77
Friends 81
God's Keeping Power 83
Gratitude 91
Fellowship 95
Seasons 99
The Heart 111
Enlargement 115

Lord of All ?..119
About The Author I

Where to Begin

You begin to walk a hundred miles, more or less, by taking the first step. You begin to write a book by writing the first sentence.

Rainbows

A word about the cover of this book. The <u>rainbow</u> is my favorite part of God's creation. Not only is it absolutely awesome and beautiful, but it symbolizes God's promises to us as individuals and as a whole in the body of Christ. When I see the rainbow, (I have a picture of one over my fireplace), it reminds me of God's promises to me every day. Only God the Creator could make something so beautiful and give meaning to it for His people.

RESTORE - **(Psalm 23: 3 - he restores my soul.**

He guides me in paths of righteousness for his name's sake).

GRACE - (2 Peter 3:18 - But grow in the grace and knowledge of our Lord and Savior Jesus Christ. To him be glory both now and forever! Amen).

The Beginning

Starting with childhood; yes, I was abused in every way possible. Will I tell you about it? No. Why? You don't need to read or hear one more sad story.

I would much rather talk about Jesus and His influence in my life. In a Baptist Sunday School class, I was introduced to Jesus for the first time at five years of age. I remember we sang "Jesus Loves Me" and then said a prayer for salvation. I saw Jesus in <u>vision form</u> and a <u>great bright light</u> around Him and He spoke to me. As I had already had a difficult childhood, I remember thinking; "Who is Jesus, and why does He love me - no one else does." He spoke to me and said "I love you." I did not fully understand the magnitude of the meaning of this experience until much later in life. (And I have never told anyone about it-until now).

A note here to anyone who ministers to children - never, ever underestimate the power of God through you when you minister to children. It is much more important than you could ever fully comprehend or imagine.

Grandmothers

Never underestimate the power and influence of a grandmother in a child's life. I lived with my grandparents for the first five years of my life, and every summer until age nine, because of WWII. My father was in Europe serving our country, and my mother lived in another town to work in a factory, making parts for WWII tanks. So I lived on a farm with my grandparents.

My grandmother loved to sing and praise Jesus while she sat and played her piano. Of course, I sat beside her and learned many of the old church hymns from her. I learned these even before going to school. Those experiences with her have given me a strong foundation in my spiritual walk. Her second passion was working in the garden around her farm. She had many, many beautiful flowers, shrubs, and trees. She also had a fruit orchard and vegetable garden. I learned to appreciate the beauty of nature that God has given us. Unfortunately, I did not inherit or develop a gardening ability. She also was an artist, sketching many pictures and painting many pictures later in life. I didn't inherit that ability either, however, one of my daughters did.

My passion, after loving and praising Jesus, is reading and writing. I'm still trying to figure out what my other talents and abilities are.

What next?

After WWII was over, my father came home and my parents and I moved to a small town not far from my grandparents. The next two years were very difficult (hell on earth). My father completely changed because of the war and could not cope with life. He and my mother were divorced after two years. I also had a baby brother born during this time. Then after two more years, my mother met and married a wonderful man who had two small girls, (his wife had died from cancer). So now, a family of six, I proceeded to belong to a family and have a normal childhood.

I was raised as a Baptist. We never missed church on Sunday. I was in the youth group and in the adult choir during my teen years, but I was not introduced into the <u>full gospel</u> circles until my late twenties. When I first saw my husband, Jerry, I saw a <u>bright white light</u> around him and knew we would marry someday. Five years later we married and had four lovely, precious, and beautiful daughters. When we purchased our first home, the instant I stepped into the entryway, I saw this <u>bright white light</u> again and knew this was our home. I did not understand these times of seeing "light" and knowing, until later when I came into the <u>full gospel</u> circles and was given the gift of "Word of Knowledge" in vision form. I began to see many things in the spirit realm, especially the <u>bright white light</u> (Jesus) and angels, and also the realm of darkness. Then I began to understand the previous experiences that I had in my life.

Compassion

My mother had polio at the age of three. At that time they did not know what they do now in the medical field. She was in the hospital every other year of her life until her teen years. They did several surgeries and therapy for her, but her leg with polio only grew to 3/4 the size of the other leg. She wore a shoe brace that went all the way up around her hip socket to give her support to walk. Her shoe was only about 3/4 the size of her other normal shoe with about a three inch wooden sole and heel to balance her walk. She never once complained or had a pity party. She had more courage, grit, and determination than anyone I've ever known. She swam, danced, walked, rode snowmobiles, and did everything else other people did. She had two children and worked for thirty years for GTE-(the telephone company), first as a telephone operator and then as an engineer in her later years. She was determined to live a normal life, and did. I really believe, watching her as I grew up, gave me a deep sense of compassion for other people. I watched her struggle every day just to try to live a normal life. As Jesus was moved with compassion to help others, that has been my heart's cry also.

Is Life Easy? No!

In my late twenties, after having four daughters and one of several major surgeries in my life, our finances began to be a problem. I thank God for this now because it drove me to seek Him with all of my being.

I read a book by Norman Vincent Peale, called "The Power of Positive Thinking". In one part he talked about a relationship with Jesus. I knew I had not experienced what he told about, so I started praying "Lord, I want that". About six months later, I had another experience with a <u>"bright</u>

white light", and I knew from then on I had a personal relationship with Jesus.

After this I started praying for a Full Gospel Church that my family and I could go to. I actually wrote a letter to The 700 Club and asked them if they knew of any churches in my area. Imagine my surprise when Pastor L. Gardner called me one Sunday afternoon (they referred my letter to him) and told me about his church of 75-100 people at that time and was about one mile from my home. I went to the Sunday evening service that evening. Pastor and his family only lived about four blocks from us.

We have been at Zion Christian Church, in Troy, Michigan, for about thirty years. God has his people every where, living and worshiping Him, and they're even closer than we can imagine. Zion Christian Church has been where God placed my family to learn and grow into maturity in

Is Life Easy? No!

the Lord. Above all else, that means growing into a closer, personal relationship with Jesus. I thank God for a pastor who always lifted Jesus up for us to see, and not man or religion. To know him(Jesus) is Eternal Life. (**John 17: 3- Now this is eternal life: that they may know you, the only true God, and Jesus Christ, whom you have sent**.) We have also been blessed greatly because Zion Christian Church has one of the most tremendous music ministries, in my opinion. Pastor Dan Gardner, known internationally for his writing and recording of worship songs to the Lord, heads the music ministry. What a blessing he and his family have been to so many people.

I believe balance is a key to walking in the Spirit. There is a poem that goes, "If you only have the Word-you will dry up; if you only have the Spirit, you will blow up; but when you have both the Word and the Spirit, you will grow up". For your spiritual health, find a church and friends who will give you both of these ingredients. Another thought on balance, most people seem to put great significance on the gifts of the Holy Spirit. While they are very important to the body of Christ, I believe that the fruit of the spirit is just as important, if not more so.(**Galatians 5: 22-23 - But the fruit of the Spirit is love, joy, peace, patience, kindness, goodness, faithfulness, gentleness and self-control. Against such things there is no law**). Can a bird fly with one wing? No. So in order to soar as the eagle and be a victorious christian, we need both the gifts and the fruit to grow (**I Corinthians 12: 8-11 - To one there is given through the Spirit the message of wisdom, to another the message of knowledge by means of the same Spirit, to another faith by the same Spirit, to another gifts of healing by that one Spirit, to another miraculous powers, to another**

prophecy, to another distinguishing between spirits, to another speaking in different kinds of tongues, and to still another the interpretation of tongues. All these are the work of one and the same Spirit, and he gives them to each one, just as he determines.) and function as an individual and as a part of the whole body of Christ **(I Corinthians 12:12 - The body is a unit, though it is made up of many parts; and though all its parts are many, they form one body. So it is with Christ.)**

I've known many wonderful Christians, some seem to have more gifts operating in their life than fruit, while others seem to have more fruit than gifts operating in their life. I believe we all need both to be mature and balanced. I don't want to be called a "flaky Christian", do you? A note here; the world is not impressed by our gifts, but they are impressed and take notice when they see the <u>character</u> of Christ in us, and the fruit of the Spirit.

The world does not need or want to see another "flash in the pan" or "shooting star" that burns bright but dies out fast. They want to see strong, mature, and well balanced Christians who know how to commune with the Lord and how to walk with him continuously. (Not up one day and down the next). Am I there yet? No!, but I'm a "work in progress", just like everyone else. There is no perfect person (other than Jesus) and there is no perfect church, simply because there are no perfect people. Didn't I tell you this book would be simple? My advice is to glean the good and positive in other peoples lives and overlook the negative.

Some Experiences

One experience I had, was while in the praise and worship part of a church service; the Lord asked me "Do you love me?". I said yes. Then He asked me "how much?". In my mind's eye, I envisioned a long horizontal line, something like a fisherman's story of how big the fish was that he caught. Then the Lord said "but, I will always love you more" and I saw Him draw a circle around my horizontal line and enclose it. The circle is like eternity and infinity, never stopping, going around and around. At this point a waterfall of tears flowed. Very profound! You can never outsmart God, so don't even try. Remember, He created you, so He knows you better than you do. He is all knowledge and all wisdom. **(Colossians 2:3 - in whom are hidden all the treasures of wisdom and knowledge).**

Another experience I had was while working in a hospital, on the 8th floor, where I was able to see the sunsets, as I worked evening hours. While looking at a spectacular sunset one evening, the Lord spoke to me, in my spirit, and said, "The Creator of the universe loves you". WOW! You could write a book on that one alone. Of course the waterfall of tears flowed again. A note here, He loves everyone with the same measure, just as much as me.

Just like a parent loves all of their children equally, so does God love all of his children. So the next time you see a beautiful sunset, remember the one who created it loves you too. [God is love and he loves his creation - us]. **(I John 4:8 - Whoever does not love does not know God, because God is love)**.

Another time as a younger Christian, I had a vision of me giving one of my small children a bath. The Lord simply said to me "Just as you wash and clean your child, because you love them, so do I wash and cleanse you because I love you". A waterfall of tears again. A note about the church. **(Ephesians 5:26 - to make her holy, cleansing her by the washing with water through the word)** - In our walk with the Lord Jesus, no matter how young or old in the Lord we are, we still need cleansing from the stains and dirt(sin) of the world.

This one I have never shared with anyone, and I don't know why. I was the leader in charge of intercessory prayer for about two years, when Zion was in the smaller church building in Clawson. One day I came to prayer (again one of many times the only one who came), very discouraged and depressed. A plain looking middle aged woman came in whom I did not recognize. The church was small enough at that time so I would have known if she went to Zion. She smiled at me and knelt to pray several feet away in another pew. Sometimes I would pray and intercede loudly, but that day I was so down that I didn't care. So I prayed very quietly and much in my thoughts. Much of my "praying" was actually questions and complaining to God. This woman, to my utter amazement, prayed out loud and began literally answering every question I was "praying" and praying scriptures in answer to my many questions and complaints to God. She could not hear me because much of my praying was in my mind or only in low whispers. But I could certainly hear her! This went on for at least one hour or longer.

The significance of the experience did not "register" with me until much later. I am completely and totally convinced she was an angel, sent by God to encourage me. "Entertain Angels Unaware". (**Hebrews 13:2 - Do not forget to entertain strangers, for by so doing some people have entertained angels without knowing it**).

Another time I was washing dishes (no dishwasher) and I noticed my neighbor working in her garden with her toddler following her around. The Lord brought the scripture (**1 Corinthians 4:15 -Even though you have ten thousand guardians in Christ, you do not have many fathers, for in Christ Jesus I became your father through the gospel**) to my mind and gave me what I call "revelation". Revelation comes in an instant of time with great understanding not known before. The Lord showed me there is need for both teachers and parents for children. We send our children to school to be taught by teachers which is very necessary. But as parents, our children learn from us as examples. They learn more by what we do than what we say. We as parents are the ones who give hugs and kisses and comfort when they are hurting. Whether it's a bandage for a cut or comfort for emotional pain, we are the ones who minister to them. So take heart and be encouraged, if you're not called to be a preacher or teacher, maybe God wants you to be a parent in the Body of Christ? Be an example - for other people are watching you.

One time when I was in college, another student asked me if I thought I was wise. What a question! My reply was, I believe there are degrees of wisdom and some people are wiser than others, and no - I did not think I was wise. But thank God, I now know the one who is and has all wisdom. All I have to do is ask God for wisdom when I need it. **(James 1:5 - If any of you lacks wisdom, he should ask God, who gives generously to all without finding fault, and it will be given to him).**

Wellspring Ministry

I was very blessed for several years to be a part of the Wellspring Ministry Committee. We organized retreats for women to go away for a weekend to a place where they could focus on Jesus and grow and learn and be ministered to. Our ministry leader, Betty Beck, although having no children of her own in the natural, I believe will be credited in heaven for many, many spiritual children. We prayed and interceded much. We worked hard on the retreats, and we had wonderful Christian fellowship with each other.

Hopefully we went home after each retreat, better and wiser Christian women. God only allowed me to be a part of the group for a few years, but what a blessing to both give and receive. All Glory and Honor to God! We had many different speakers through the years, too many to count and name, who ministered the word and prayed with all the women. Some are known nationally and some internationally. What a privilege and honor to be a part of this one small area of God's great work. That was one of many "seasons" in my life. Now God says, "I'm in a season for writing". After this, only God knows. He guides and directs, but only one step at a time, or one page of our life at a time.

Unity

Once the Lord gave me a vision of many, many people drowning in a large body of water (symbolic of the unsaved). There were many, many Christians standing all around the shore of this great body of water, arguing over which one was their's to save, while "they were drowning". Another waterfall of tears flowed and I had a deep aching in my heart. Can you imagine how sad and displeased our Lord must be?

We are called to live in unity! (**Psalms 133:1-3 - A**

song of ascents. Of David. How good and pleasant it is when brothers live together in unity It is like precious oil poured on the head, running down on the beard, running down on Aaron's beard, down upon the collar of his robes. It is as if the dew of Hermon were falling on Mount Zion. For there the LORD bestows his blessing, even life forevermore). This brings God's blessings. If we bite and devour one another with jealousy, who has what title, and one-up manship, we are not in unity and will soon destroy one another. (**Galatians 5:15 - If you keep on biting and devouring each other, watch out or you will be destroyed by each other**). Is it not time to grow up and be mature and live in unity? How much faster and smoother the Lord's work could be done if we simply put away childish attitudes and ways. (**1 Corinthians 13:11 - When I was a child, I talked like a child, I thought like a child, I reasoned like a**

child. When I became a man, I put childish ways behind me). How many more people could be saved.

We seem to forget sometimes, that God has a purpose and destiny for each one of us. If we could only comprehend this principle and do what our Lord tells each of us to do, and not be concerned with someone else's walk with the Lord. (**2 Corinthians 10:12 -We do not dare to classify or compare ourselves with some who commend themselves. When they measure themselves by themselves and compare themselves with themselves, they are not wise).** Be obedient and do what He tells you to do and pray for others that they may do the same in their life. No condemnation is meant to be directed here, but instead an encouragement to seek the Lord and His will for you and a prayer that we will all walk in obedience as He directs us.

The Vine - Jesus

(John 15:5 - "I am the vine; you are the branches. If a man remains in me and I in him, he will bear much fruit; apart from me you can do nothing). Apart from Jesus, you can do nothing, at least not for any eternal significance. Any discord in the body of Christ will sever that connection. Any gossip, jealousy, negative talking, comparison with others, etc., will separate us from our source: Jesus the vine, and we will be ineffective Christians.

I pray no one (including me) allows this to happen to

them, and if and when we realize we have lost our connection to our source, Jesus, all we have to do is repent and we will be restored again instantly. (**Acts 3:19 - Repent, then, and turn to God, so that your sins may** be **wiped out, that times of refreshing may come from the Lord**).

Only by staying in the place of communion with the Lord, spending time daily in prayer and in the Word, can we stay connected to our source, Jesus (the vine). It is a discipline that we must embrace if we want to grow into mature Christians in the Lord. When we go through the hard and difficult times in our lives, it is even more imperative for us to discipline ourselves. We may not feel like it or even want to, but we will suffer in our spiritual life if we neglect this principle.

In the midst of our trials and tribulations, we need to be connected to our source, Jesus, more than ever. It not only affects us, but also affects the many people, whose lives

we touch every day

You, Again?

I choose to focus on Jesus, especially in writing this book, but I must touch lightly on the fact that there is an enemy of our souls that we must deal with if we are to triumph and walk in victory. Like weeds in a garden, we must take care of; but choose to focus on the flowers and beauty.

I learned once from an older dear saint, Nan Hunt, in a series of prayer meetings, that she simply never invited the devil. She would go to the throne room with Father God in the simplicity of a child. The greatest insult to someone is to ignore them! She simply ignored the devil and only talked to Father God. If the devil had the audacity to show up uninvited, she simply rebuked him in the Name of Jesus and he left. And as she prayed for others, only when necessary did she rebuke the devil and apply the blood of Jesus to that person's life. A note to the intercessors of the world. I am an intercessor and fully understand we must do warfare in prayer; sometimes very strongly and sometimes fasting is needed. But my point is that we should focus on Jesus and not the enemy in our prayer meetings. There is deception in thinking we always need to war in the spirit realm. It is a trick and strategy of the devil to take our focus off Jesus and the prayers for other's needs and circumstances. It is as simple as turning on a light in a room. The darkness is dispelled instantly. **(John 1:5 - The light (Jesus) shines in the darkness, but the darkness has not understood**

(overcome) it).

When and if the Lord shows you an area of darkness in another saint's life, pray for the person and rebuke the devil absolutely, but don't tell that person when the Lord reveals these things to you. Only pray! Give love and encouragement as the Lord directs and simply pray until you are assured that the darkness has left that person. Pray for God's grace, love, and mercy to be poured into their life. How these qualities are brought into that person's life is God's business. Line upon line, precept upon precept (**KJV-Isaiah 28:10 - For precept must be upon precept, precept upon precept; line upon line, line upon line; here a little, and there a little**). The Lord will cause the dark areas in a person's life to be dispelled in His timing. Our part is to pray! (Till Christ be formed in you).(**Galatians 4:19 - My dear children, for whom I am am in the pains of child**

birth (travail) **until Christ is formed in you**).

Remember, we all are "a work in progress." Only God, the Potter, (**KJV - Jeremiah 18:6 -O house of Israel, cannot I do with you as this potter? saith the LORD. Behold, as the clay is in the potter's hand, so are ye in mine hand, O house of Israel**), knows exactly what He is doing and what the finished product will be. We think we do sometimes, but we don't in our lives or in other's lives.

I could tell you of many encounters that I have had with the devil, but all Christians go through this and it's different for everyone simply because we are all very different from each other. God created us that way. I will say the devil knows God wants to use each one of us so you can be assured he will come against you again and again and try to stop you from being prepared for and used as vessel for God's purpose and will. Does he ever stop trying? Unfortunately no.

He will leave for a season, but always comes back. A lesson here in perseverance! Because he is a created being, just as we are, Hello! (revelation here), that means God's abilities, knowledge, wisdom, etc., are so much greater in magnitude, than our's or the devil's. So why would we not choose to focus on the Lord, Jehovah, Creator of all and worship Him and ignore the devil?

I am not trying to diminish the power and influence of the devil; but only choose to focus on God and worship Him in Spirit and Truth and in the Spirit of holiness.(**John 4:23 - Yet a time is coming and has now come when the true worshipers will worship the Father in spirit and truth, for they are the kind of worshipers the Father seeks).**

When we learn to walk in the light of God's presence on a continous basis, our walk becomes easier. The devil hates the presence of God and will not come near it. But he will try every one of his tactics and strategies to keep us from walking in God's light and presence.

The eagle soars higher than any other bird. When attacked, they simply mount up higher and higher until they reach an altitude in which their enemies cannot survive. They do not waste time battling with other birds that are pests to them. A lesson here. When the devil comes your way, simply mount up on wings of praise and worship to God and come into His presence, and the devil will soon leave you alone, Our walk with our Lord Jesus can be very simple and joyful and peaceful. In our humanity, we seem to want to make if difficult and complex.

A brief word on the occult, which most people know and understand is the realm of darkness, where the devil rules. Do I know anything about this? Yes! When I was in my twenties, I "delved" into several areas of the occult, in my ignorance. Astrology was the most interesting to me. I even studied and took classes. I could chart someone's life by the position of the planets at their birth and at the present time in their life (and tell their future); which we seem to be so fascinated with as humans. I could tell you your rising sign, sun sign, planet and moon placements, etc., which of course all supposedly meant something. Why am I telling you this? For two reasons. First, why on earth would we choose to worship something created instead of the Creator, Jehovah God? That I have learned and embraced completely! Second, I needed prayer after becoming a Christian (born-again) to renounce and get rid of the "influence" in my life. I also repented and have prayed for the many people whose lives I touched with this evil influence. Again the light and power of Jesus dispels one more area of darkness in my life. A note here. Some people believe a persons life can be influenced by someone in your past family background who moved in these areas of the devil's domain and influence. My advice is to seek God on your own or go to a spiritual leader to see if you need prayer for release of this influence in your life. Only God knows if you do!

(Jesus is the way, the truth, and the life - John 14: 6) Someone once told me that people who work in banks and handle money continuously learn to know the counterfeit bills by handling the real bills continuously, so that when the counterfeit comes along, they know it instantly. What a lesson to apply to the Spiritual realm! If you dwell and walk in the light and presence of Jesus on a continuous basis: when the counterfeit (the devil) comes along: you will discern him instantly.

Another lesson here. The devil seeks to counterfeit

everything of God. Whether it is false teaching, or false gifts, etc., there can be great deception. All the more reason to walk so close to our Lord Jesus and dwell in His light and presence so we will not be deceived. (**Matthew 24:24 - For false Christs and false prophets will appear and perform great signs and miracles to deceive even the elect--if that were possible**). Even the very elect can be deceived if they are not very careful. Enough for now about the realm of darkness. Like I said before; I prefer to focus on Jesus and dwell in His light and presence.

Joy

Why write about Joy? Because it seems to me that so many Christians lack the joy that is their God given right and inheritance. The joy of the Lord is our strength. God meets with those who rejoice. Rejoice evermore not sometimes, but always - (**Philippians 4:4 - Rejoice in the Lord always. I will say it again: Rejoice**!) The fruit of the Spirit is mentioned in Galatians 5:22 (Love is first). Have I always had the joy of the Lord? No!! Just ask my family and friends.

Joy is not necessarily in what we have or want; and

different from happiness. Joy to me is like a deep perpetual spring within us that is always there for us to draw upon, **(Isaiah 12:3 - With joy you will draw water from the wells of salvation)**. The choice is ours - to be joyful or not. This is not meant to take away from real sorrow and grief from the loss of a loved one or something dear to us in life. There are different seasons in everyone's life. But we can still have deep peace and joy in our hearts when going through seasons of pain and suffering. God will be there to comfort us (**2 Corinthians 1:3 - Praise be to the God and Father of our Lord Jesus Christ, the Father of compassion and the God of all comfort**), and to restore peace and joy. "He is faithful always."

The first miracle of Jesus was turning water into wine at the wedding feast of Cana. (**John 2: 7-9 - Jesus said to the servants, "Fill the jars with water"; so they filled**

them to the brim .Then he told them, "Now draw some out and take it to the master of the banquet." They did so, and the master of the banquet tasted the water that had been turned into wine. He did not realize where it had come from, though the servants who had drawn the water knew). Water symbolizes the word and wine symbolizes the joy of the Lord. Notice, only when the water was poured out did it become joy. A lesson here on selfishness, self-centeredness, and self-pity. Start pouring into other's lives what God has given you and what you have learned from the Word (Jesus) and you will find joy of effervescence overflowing in your life.

A Word To The Unsaved

(and to those who think they are; but are not)

If you understand that title, you are already, definitely saved. If you do not, you might want to read this chapter. I grew up in a Baptist church and assumed I was saved. I found out in my late twenties I was not. What a shock! It is called "giving mental belief". If you believe in your mind, but not in your heart, you have not truly been born-again by the Holy Spirit of God. (**Romans 10:9 -That if you confess with your mouth, "Jesus is Lord," and believe in your**

heart that God raised him from the dead, you will be saved).

To anyone who is not sure that you are saved, please pray the following prayer:

> Dear God, I know I am a sinner and unable to save myself. But I do believe you love me, and that you sent your son Jesus to die on the cross for my sins. Right here and now, Lord Jesus, I repent of my sins and invite you to come into my heart, forgive my every sin, and grant me your gift of eternal life. Thank you dear Lord for hearing and answering my prayer, and for coming into my heart and life, as you promised you would. Amen.

It took many years for me to convince my mother, who believed she was saved because she went to the altar and said a sinner's prayer when she was younger. But I knew she had not truly been born again by the Spirit of God when I prayer for her.

In God's timing, she did come to the realization and

true experience of salvation. When you receive Jesus as your savior; literally into your heart, you become a new person.(**II Corinthians 5:17 - Therefore, if anyone is in Christ, he is a new creation; the old has gone, the new has come!**). You know it and so do others! You may or may not grow into adulthood and maturity in the spirit life, but the choice is yours! It's not easy to grow up into spiritual maturity. It's easier to stay in the baby stage or childhood stage. But if you want to come into God's purpose and destiny for your life - you will choose to grow up. It can be a painful process, but well worth the effort. You would not want to remain a baby or child in the natural realm, so why would you want to in the spiritual realm? To please God and become an effective Christian, we should choose to grow up.

Pride-Who Me?

Pride, I believe is one of the greatest sins in God's sight, if not the worst. Lucifer's (devil) was pride - he thought he could be greater than God (Isaiah 14: 12-14). Hello! Remember he's a created being just as the angels and us.

When I was a younger Christian, many people told me I was a very humble person, so I began to believe I was. Actually, I was just shy and quiet. What a shock, when one day the Holy Spirit revealed to me I had pride. Ouch! Didn't really want to hear that. We can have pride in many ways and in many things. Only the Lord can show us if and in what area of our life we do have it. Pride in giftings, in titles, in doing good deeds, in being an active Christian, in never missing church, in never speaking negatively (although we might think negatively in our hearts). Man, (Hello!) does not see our heart - but guess who does? (**I Samuel 16:7 - But the LORD said to Samuel, "Do not consider his appearance or his height, for I have rejected him. The LORD does not look at the things man looks at. Man looks at the outward appearance, but the LORD looks at the heart"**).

God is much more interested in our hearts, attitudes and motives, than in what we say and do, or how we appear to others. He is interested in the <u>why</u> of what we say and do. Is it to please Him and be obedient and bring Him glory; or is it to please man and appear to be "spiritual"? Only God can tell you.

Mirrors

The <u>mirror</u> that we choose to look into is essential and of vital importance. We can choose to look into the mirror of the Word and see ourselves as God sees us, and be a victorious Christian bearing fruit in God's kingdom, or we can choose to look into our own mirror and see ourselves only as we see ourselves. This can be very dangerous, because we tend to see ourselves incorrectly. The image is often distorted and not the whole truth. We can see ourselves in a puffed up and prideful way which is a deception. Or we can see ourselves at the opposite end of the spectrum, as much less than what God intends for us to be, which is also a deception. (**Jeremiah 17:9-10 - The heart is deceitful above all things and beyond cure. Who can understand it? "I the LORD search the heart and examine the mind, to reward a man according to his conduct, according to what his deeds deserve**"). The third mirror can tie in very closely with the mirror of how we see ourselves. The devil likes nothing better than to feed us lies and distort God's truth about us. He can cause us to stumble and fall just by lying to us about how we appear to ourselves and to each other or to God. He can bring us condemnation (**Romans 8:1 -Therefore, there is now no condemnation for those who are in Christ Jesus**) by accusing us to ourselves and before Father God. He can cause us to think we are a high mountain (pride), or a very low valley (condemnation) which are both distorted and deceptive lies.(**John 8:44 -You belong to your father, the devil, and you want to carry out your father's desire. He was a murderer from the beginning, not holding to the truth, for there is no truth in him. When he lies, he speaks his native language, for he is a liar and the father of lies**).

The answer is to look always into the mirror of God's word (truth) and see ourselves as God sees us. As soon as we turn from (**2 Corinthians 3:18 - And we, who with unveiled faces all reflect the Lord's glory, are being transformed into his likeness with ever- increasing glory, which comes from the Lord, who is the Spirit**) looking into God's mirror, we get into trouble. A note here. God sees us through the blood of Jesus and His righteousness and always as King's kids whom He loves with an eternal, everlasting love.

However, sometimes when we are looking into God's mirror (Word), we will see things by revelation of the Holy Spirit of God and know that God wants to change us. Because of His great love for us, this will always be for our good and His glory, but the process can be painful. (Growth is not always easy, but is the best way).

God, being the <u>master potter</u> (**Jeremiah 18:6 - "O house of Israel, can I not do with you as this potter does?" declares the LORD. "Like clay in the hand of the potter, so are you in my hand, O house of Israel**), always knows exactly what He is doing and what end result He is aiming for in shaping and molding us into His image. He also sits as a refiner of precious metal (**Malachi 3:3 -He will sit as a refiner and purifier of silver; he will purify the Levites and refine them like gold and silver. Then the LORD will have men who will bring offerings in righteousness**). When we are going through difficult times and we think we're not going to make it, we often want to throw in the towel and give up and quit. This is when we need to remember God is only out to do us good and wants to create a beautiful vessel (**II Timothy 2:21 -If a man cleanses himself from the latter, he will be an instrument for noble purposes, made holy, useful to the Master and prepared to do any good work**) that He can use. The dross which the refiner takes away is only a person, circumstance, attitude, motive, or something that would be unfruitful ,and not good for us.

Glorify God in the fires (**KJV Isaiah 24:15 - Wherefore glorify ye the LORD in the fires, even the name of the LORD God of Israel in the isles of the sea**), which are the hard and difficult times in our lives. We shall come forth as gold and silver, cleansed and shining brighter than ever before if we will yield and allow Him to do His work in us.

A note here. We are given a free will by God. His is always a gentleman and never forces us to do anything. We may not have control over who we are, our parents, our circumstances, etc., but we always have the free will to choose how to react and respond. The choices are always ours. Isn't God awesome and magnificent to allow His creation the free will to choose to love Him in return for His unconditional love and to choose to be changed into His image?

There is no other way or choice to the Christian who loves the Lord and wants to please Him and bring glory to Him from his or her life (**Isaiah 61:3 - They will be called oaks of righteousness, a planting of the LORD for the display of his splendor**). May we never forget that God is loving, good, merciful, gracious, and is always working His good purpose into our lives and for His glory.(**Romans 8:28 -And we know that in all hings God works for the good** of those who love him, who have been called according to his purpose).

Memories

I love the scripture - (**Psalms 103:12 - as far as the east is from the west, so far has he removed our transgressions from us**). God chooses to not only forgive but forget our sins; when we repent. Here again comes the free will to choose. We can choose to believe God's word (truth) or we can believe the lies of the devil who continuously likes to remind us of our sins, weaknesses, and mistakes; (notice all negative).

Sometimes we even like to help the devil along and

we become allies with him in our thoughts and words of condemnation, against ourselves and others. This can be very dangerous, leading to worse things like depression, oppression, self-pity, etc. But here again is that free will our Father God has given us to choose whether to believe God's truth (word) about ourselves or to believe the lies of the devil and even help him along in pulling us down.

When we wake up in the morning, we can actually <u>choose</u> to have a great day in the Lord, or we can choose to think and speak negatively and have a bad day. Regardless of our circumstances, or even pain, fatigue, and suffering in our physical bodies, we still have the free will to choose what kind of day we're going to have. I personally find that fascinating! Have I always chosen correctly? No! But remember I'm still a work in progress and on the Potter's wheel and so are you! If you always choose correctly; God bless you for being so perfect. Maybe you could write a book and teach the rest of us how to be so perfect. (A little sarcasm here-maybe God has a great deal of work to do in me yet). I hope you find this humorous, because I do.

As Pastor Gardner's son, Pastor Don would say when he was preaching, ("if you're not enjoying this; it doesn't really matter because I'm preaching myself happy" - that is freedom). So I'm writing myself happy! If you're enjoying the book, great. If not, it doesn't really matter to me because I have joy and am being obedient to Father. I do write this in love for you, however.

We all have memories in our memory banks. Some of us, by reason of age have a larger memory bank. Here again we have the free will to choose to dwell on the past (whether good or bad memories) or dwell and focus on the present and look to the future with hope. (**Jeremiah 29:**

11 - For I know the plans I have for you," declares the LORD, "plans to prosper you and not to harm you, plans to give you hope and a future). We should choose to live in the present tense and focus on Jesus, enjoy the life God has given us - (and look to the future with hope). When we choose to focus on the past or worry about the future, we are not enjoying life in the present. I believe our loving Heavenly Father wants us to <u>enjoy</u> life. We do that by keeping our eyes on Jesus (**Hebrews 12:2 - Let us fix our eyes on Jesus, the author and perfecter of our faith, who for the joy set before him endured the cross, scorning its shame, and sat down at the right hand of the throne of God**) and seeking God's will through prayer and His word on a daily basis and then we can walk in joy and peace. The devil comes to steal, kill, and destroy (**John 10:10 - The thief comes only to steal and kill and destroy; I have come that they may**

have life, and have it to the full). He can do that by robbing us of our present daily life of joy in the Lord. When the devil can get us to focus on the past and worry or fret about the future, he causes us to lose our <u>victory</u> in the present. (**1 Corinthians 15:57 - But thanks be to God! He gives us the victory through our Lord Jesus Christ**).

Thank God for the Holy Spirit, the one called alongside us to help us and comfort us and direct us. All we have to do is pray and ask for help when we need it. (**John 14:26 - But the Counselor,and Comforter,the Holy Spirit, whom the Father will send in my name, will teach you all things and will remind you of everything I have said to you**).

Encouragement

I believe encouragement is one of the most important elements in the Body of Christ. (**Acts 4:36 - Joseph, a Levite from Cyprus, whom the apostles called Barnabas -which means Son of Encouragement**). His very name means "one that encourages". Sometimes just a smile can lift someone's spirit and cause them to feel better. Encouragement comes in many ways. It can be through a card in the mail. It can be a positive, cheerful statement to someone. It can even be in saying "I've been praying for you". It can come through Christian music and the Word. If the Body of Christ would take time to encourage one another much more than done already; I believe we would all be spiritually stronger. It can be a visit to the hospital or someone who is home bound with illness, or in prison. (**Matthew 25: 34-36 - "Then the King will say to those on his right, 'Come, you who are blessed by my Father; take your inheritance, the kingdom prepared for you since the creation of the world. For I was hungry and you gave me something to eat, I was thirsty and you gave me something to drink, I was a stranger and you invited me in, I needed clothes and you clothed me, I was sick and you looked after me, I was in prison and you came to visit me**). It can be a phone call. It can be money given (but only as directed by the Lord). It can be a hug and or a prayer with someone. It can be given in helping anyone with a need. Some people are given the gift of helps, (**1 Corinthians 12:28 - And in the church God has appointed first of all apostles, second prophets, third teachers, then workers of miracles, also those having gifts of healing, those able to help others, those with gifts of administration, and those speaking in different kinds of tongues**) by the Lord. What a blessing they are to the Body of Christ. But I believe we can all become <u>better</u> encouragers of each other and we would all profit and grow spiritually.

Even David had to encourage himself in the Lord (**KJV-1 Samuel 30:6 - And David was greatly distressed; for the people spake of stoning him, because the soul of all the people was grieved, every man for his sons and for his daughters: but David encouraged himself in the LORD his God**). And in scripture: Paul said, "But the Lord stood with me". That's the greatest encouragement, just to know that God is always with us and for us. But how much better, if we could also learn and take time to encourage one another, as the Lord leads. The key here is simple obedience.

When the Holy Spirit impresses us to pray for someone, maybe we should also do something to encourage them. Here we need to pray and ask for God's leading and direction. Sometimes God wants us just to pray. He may be doing a work in that person's heart. Maybe He wants them to seek Him more and not go to man if they are so inclined. Encouragement comes sometimes as "songs in the night" **(Psalms 42:8 - By day the LORD directs his love, at night his song is with me-- a prayer to the God of my life).** given by God or dreams, visions, etc.

A word about "checks in the spirit". Sometimes we will have a check in our spirit about saying or doing something. An older saint was asked once by a younger, newer Christian -"What is your secret to living in spiritual victory?" Her answer was simple. "Mind the Checks!" I believe this is something we each learn as we walk with the Lord. We need to be sensitive to the impressions the Holy Spirit would give us. A check in your spirit means "NO". Even if you think all seems right in your mind. Trust me, if you get a check in your spirit, stop immediately. Don't say or do what you had planned to. This will save you a great deal of pain and suffering or making wrong choices and mistakes. Sometimes it also affects others negatively. A note here. After a younger, newer Christian experiences this a few times, if you're a fast learner (quick study), you will soon learn to know when you are being checked in your spirit.

Spiritual Leaders

Am I an authority on the subject? No! But just a few thoughts and lessons that I have learned. The only way I believe, to approach this subject, is to go the the Word, which is the God given authority concerning it. (**Ephesians 4: 11-12 - It was he who gave some to be apostles, some to be prophets, some to be evangelists, and some to be pastors and teachers, to prepare God's people for works of service, so that the body of Christ may be built up**). God gave some apostles, some prophets, some evangelists, some pastors, and teachers; for the perfecting of the saints, for the work of the ministry, and for the edifying of the Body of Christ. Also elders and deacons are given to the Body of Christ. Are leaders perfect? No! Because they are people too, who are also a work in progress, just like us. But according to the Word, we are to give them honor and respect, because of the office they hold. They are placed there by God and if and when He chooses to remove them for whatever reason, that is His business, not ours! Our responsibility is to come under their authority in the Body of Christ and also to pray for them. If we think we see or know of a fault or sin in their lives, we should, I believe, only pray and let God take care of it. As long as you are where God has placed you, follow the rules according to the word. (**1 Timothy 2: 1-2 - I urge, then, first of all, that requests, prayers, intercession and thanksgiving be made for everyone-for kings and all those in authority, that we may live peaceful and quiet lives in all godliness and holiness**). Also the leaders set in authority, by God, are the spiritual covering in the Body of Christ. When we do not check out the Word and be obedient to it, I believe we open the door to the devil to bring us confusion and deception.

I have learned a few lessons the hard way. Am I going to share them with you? No! Suffice to say, I would have saved myself much pain and suffering had I been obedient to the Word. If you simply cannot come to peaceful terms with someone in authority over you, maybe you should pray and seek God. He might tell you to join another body of believers in the Body of Christ. A note here. My advice to you is to seek God humbly and wholeheartedly; for the problem just might be with you. Ouch!! Didn't want to hear that! If you don't allow God to change you, (if you have the problem), you simply take the same problem with you to another body of believers and go around the same mountain again. Hello! A lesson here. I call these people tumbleweeds, blowing around from place to place with no direction and never becoming rooted and grounded in the Word. **(Ephesians 3: 16-18- I pray that out of his glorious riches he may strengthen you with power through his Spirit in your inner being so that Christ may dwell in your hearts through faith. And I pray that you, being rooted and established in love, may have power, together with all the**

saints, to grasp how wide and long and high and deep is the love of Christ).

My prayer is to become an oak tree; strongly rooted and grounded wherever God chooses to plant and place me. **(Isaiah 61:3 - They will be called oaks of righteousness, a planting of the LORD for the display of his splendor).**

A note here. There are times when God will move a Christian to another place, in His will and purpose for their life. If this happens, there should be peace and unity in the transition stage. We can be placed in one body of believers for a season of learning and giving, and then God might move us on to another body of believers to learn more and/or to give out of what we have learned. But only God knows the times and seasons and if we are to move. Seek God and pray much. **(1 Thessalonians 5:17 - pray continually).**

Friends

There is a friend who is closer than a brother (**Proverbs 17:17 - A friend loves at all times, and a brother is born for adversity**). Sometimes we form very strong bonds between our brothers and sisters in the Lord, even stronger than natural family ties. God blesses us with wonderful Christian friends if we are open and want it. Will they always be perfect and never fail us? No! Only God will always be faithful to us. One of my favorite songs is "What a Friend we have in Jesus". But there is also great joy in having Christian friends. Some are closer to us than others. Sometimes God orders this and sometimes, I believe, it's a personality thing. We seem to bond with some people more quickly and easier than others. Only God knows why. A true friend is someone you can call in the middle of the night with an urgent need. I'm not talking about acquaintances or people who pass through your life for a brief time.

A friend will laugh with you when you laugh and cry (and pray) with you when you cry. They will lend a listening ear when you need it and hopefully you can do the same for them. They will love you when others don't and overlook your faults and weaknesses. Most important, they will hear from God if need be for you. They will love you, even if they don't understand you. If you're like me, you don't even understand yourself sometimes. Only God really understands us. Hello! Remember, he created us.

God's Keeping Power

I believe the devil tries to steal, kill and destroy all of us, some more than others. **(Jude 24 -To him who is able to keep you from falling and to present you before his glorious presence without fault and with great joy--).** Why? Simply, because he knows God wants to use each and every one of us as His chosen, anointed, and powerful vessels to give Him glory. We are not only saved by grace, but we are kept by the power of God and He will not allow the devil to destroy us. We go to the throne of grace by prayer to find grace and mercy in our times of need. (**Hebrews 4:16 - Let us therefore come boldly unto the throne of grace, that we may obtain mercy, and find grace to help in time of need).** We walk in daily God given strength by the power of God's grace. We deal with people and circumstances daily by God's grace. All we have to do is ask God for grace and mercy and He gives it abundantly to us, his children. **(Lamentations 3:22-23 - Because of the Lord's great love we are not consumed, for his compassions never fail. They are new every morning; great is your faithfulness).** There are many people in scripture who were restored by God's grace, mercy, love, and power. Just study the life of Joseph! God's grace kept him through betrayal by his jealous brothers; by Potiphor's wife's seduction; by being in prison and even forgotten by others. But God had a purpose and destiny for Joseph, not only to keep and restore his life, but to use it for His glory. I believe Joseph trusted God and His grace completely through his many trials and temptations. But look at the end result. **(Genesis 50:20 - But as for you, ye thought evil against me; but God meant it unto good, to bring to pass, as it is this day, to save much people alive).** All glory went to God and Joseph and his people were kept and restored by God's grace.

Another example is Ruth. She chose to trust the God of Naomi, her mother-in-law. She also took counsel from her and trusted her wisdom as an elder to her. The end result was restoration for Ruth, Naomi, and her seed through Boaz. This of course was the lineage of Christ. God is a God of grace and restoration again and again through His word, and also in our lives.

Look at Job. God allowed the devil to meddle in Job's life and rob him of almost everything he had. But the end result? God gave Job double for what was taken away from him. Our words; what we speak are very important in God's sight. God answered Job's prayers for his friends because he spoke what was right about God. **(Job 42:7).**

Another example is Esther. She was obedient and trusted God. She even risked her life for herself and her people. The end result? Again, restoration and God got the glory.

Daniel trusted God even in the lion's den. Shadrach, Meshach, and Abednego trusted God in the fiery furnace and refused to worship any other god than the Most High God. The end result? Restoration and God received the glory again! He always will!

Another example is Paul in the New Testament. God completely restored his life and God received all the glory. Paul as a man used by the enemy first, but then by God, for

His glory.

Jesus is the best example. Study His life in the New Testament. He went through much more pain and suffering than any of us ever will or can even imagine. God restored him completely! He sits on the right hand of Father God. **(Hebrews 12:2 - Looking unto Jesus the author and finisher of our faith; who for the joy that was set before him endured the cross, despising the shame, and is set down at the right hand of the throne of God).** Jesus was obedient unto the Father, even to death on the cross. The devil thought he could destroy Jesus on the cross. Not too smart! But Jesus rose from the grave triumphant in power and glory. Again God receives all the glory.

By and through the shed blood of Jesus on the cross of calvary, we can be restored completely, and walk in victory daily. We are saved and born again instantly by receiving Jesus as our Savior. But to grow in grace and in the knowledge of Jesus Christ and to be restored by grace, is a life long process.

It constantly amazes me that God can use us from day one of being saved, even when we are not restored completely. Remember, it's a life long process, but God can receive glory from any one of us, as his children, no matter whether we are a new Christian or a "seasoned veteran" Christian.

When you think you're having a bad day or week, just stop and think about what Jesus went through. These are just some of the things He suffered: in Isaiah chapter 53, He had no form or beauty, that when we see Him we would desire him. He was despised and rejected of men; a man of sorrows; acquainted with grief and not appreciated. He was wounded, bruised, chastised, and stripes were cut on His back. He was oppressed, afflicted, and as a lamb brought to slaughter; yet He opened not His mouth. He was punished for our trangressions. Do you still think you're having a bad day or week?(**Hebrews 12:3-4 For consider him that endured such contradiction of sinners against himself, lest ye be wearied and faint in your minds. Ye have not yet resisted unto blood, striving against sin).** Despising the shame of the cross, he endured it out of His love for us. When Jesus was in the Garden of Gethsemane, He resisted unto blood. Have you ever resisted unto blood? I surely haven't. I don't know anyone who has.

Gratitude

An attitude of gratitude or thanksgiving is key to a victorious walk with our Lord. We cannot even come into his presence without it. **(Psalm 100:4 - Enter into his gates with thanksgiving, and into his courts with praise: be thankful unto him, and bless his name).** A grateful and thankful heart is very pleasing to the Lord. Even answered prayers are vital to having a thankful heart. When we <u>choose</u> to be grateful and satisfied with what God has already blessed us with, then we are opening the door to greater blessings being out-poured. However, if we <u>choose</u> to murmur and complain and not be grateful, then we close the door to blessings. We not only close the door, but all of the friends of ingratitude feel they're invited; such as self-pity, selfishness, oppression, depression, discouragement, etc. I'm sure you get the idea.

When we choose to dwell in God's presence with a thankful heart and walk in obedience, His blessings will not only come to us but they will over take us. (**Deuteronomy 28:2 - And all these blessings shall come on thee, and overtake thee, if thou shalt hearken unto the voice of the LORD thy God).** Would you rather be around someone who is thankful and cheerful, or who is negative and always in self-pity, and with a complaining and murmuring spirit? I'm sure most people would choose the first one, although misery does love company. Ouch! A little too much reality?

Birds of a feather flock together! Who hasn't heard that saying? We can learn agreat deal about ourselves by the company of friends we choose to be with. I once heard a speaker say, "Listen to what comes out of your mouth" and you will know how far your spiritual growth has come. I also heard a speaker say once that if we can only receive compliments and praise, but not fair criticism and some negative input, we will not grow very fast in the Spirit. We need to take any criticism or judging to the Lord in prayer and ask with an open mind, "Is this true Lord?" If He says "no", we can trash it. But if He says "yes", then continue praying that he will help us change in that area. Another ouch! Growing up spiritually is definitely not without some growth pains. Do we want the easy way or the difficult? Do we want to live in the comfort zone or grow up? I pray for you and for myself; that we <u>choose</u> to grow up, no matter how painful the process.

Even Jesus, our example, gave thanks much in prayer. Jesus gave thanks in prayer at the last supper, knowing He would be betrayed by Judas and knowing He was facing death on the cross by crucifiction. Some of us can't even give thanks for simple every day things that are positive, let alone negative.

We're commanded to give thanks in prayer. We are commanded to give thanks in trials; not for, but in them. The trials go faster and smoother with a spirit of thanksgiving and praise.

Fellowship

We are commanded to have fellowship; first with the Father, Son, and Holy Spirit. Then, second, we are to have fellowship with other Christians. God listens to our words carefully when we are in fellowship with one another. Sharing the Word, our experiences, and sharing our needs in prayer are all included. We are told to rejoice with those who rejoice and mourn with those who mourn. **(Romans 12:15 - Rejoice with them that do rejoice, and weep with them that weep).**

We are not only called to rejoice in fellowship with other Christians, but also to fellowship with them when they are going through difficult times in their lives. Through simple love and caring for them; by visitation, prayers, phone calls, cards, etc., we can encourage and fellowship with them. In blessing, we will be blessed. Isn't God good? We cannot out give Him. When we give to Him, He pours manifold blessings to us, and when we give to others, we are blessed many times over: by God, not always man. Remember who our real source is, God!

One of the dearest saints I know is an older saint who gives and gives of her time and energy to the poor and homeless in the inner city of Detroit. She is part of a group who ministers to, and feeds and gives clothing to the needy. She has more joy and energy than most saints that I know. (Georgia Elliot). A lesson here. Giving to others brings much joy to us and also to Father God.

Fellowship can be one on one, like just having a cup of coffee with someone. Or it can be in larger groups and in church. However God chooses to direct us to fellowship with others is His business. Often it is with those who are in the same type of ministry as we are. A word here about having fellowship only with those we like to be around. If God leads us to be with people who are not exactly the way we'd like, maybe He is trying to do a work in our heart or even in theirs. We need to be sensitive to His leading and open to embrace new people and people who are different from us.

About mentors. Sometimes we are mentored by someone else, especially as newer Christians. We can also be used as mentors for others as God leads us. The Body of Christ needs more mentors, people who will take time to help others to grow spiritually and understand spiritual things better.

This is not new to most Christians, but I will inject it here for those who may not have heard it. Christian fellowship can be compared to many, many live burning coals on a grill. When together, they stay hot with zeal and energy. But when one is off to the side and away from the others, they can become cold very fast with little life and energy, let alone zeal. A great lesson here. **(Hebrews 10:25 - Not forsaking the assembling of ourselves together, as the manner of some is; but exhorting one another: and so much the more, as ye see the day approaching).** Neglect not the assembling of ourselves, and stay in fellowship, one with another.

Seasons

There are many different seasons in the life of a Christian. **(Ecclesiastes 3:1-8 - To every thing there is a season, and a time to every purpose under the heaven: A time to be born, and a time to die; A time to plant, and a time to pluck up that which is planted; A time to kill, and a time to heal; a time to break down, and a time to build up; A time to weep, and a time to laugh; A time to mourn, and a time to dance; A time to cast away stones, and a time to gather stones together; A time to embrace,**

and a time to refrain from embracing; A time to get, and a time to lose; a time to keep, and a time to cast away; A time to rend, and a time to sew; a time to keep silence, and a time to speak; A time to love, and a time to hate; a time of war, and a time of peace).

Sometimes we are in the desert for a season; a long dry time of not being aware of God's voice and His presence. Has He deserted us? No! His promise is "I will never leave you nor forsake you". **(Hebrews 13:5 - Let your conversation be without covetousness; and be content with such things as ye have: for he hath said, I will never leave thee, nor forsake thee).** But He allows us to go through a season of time in the desert. When we come out, always in God's perfect timing, we will be renewed and refreshed by the rain of His presence and the water of the Word. And most important, we will have learned an important lesson that God is teaching us. All Christians have these times of desert dryness in their lives, however we feel alone and like we're the only one going through it.

Another season is when we go through the valley. Trust me; we all go through these times. It may be the loss of a loved one through death. It may be the loss of someone or something that causes a brokenheart. **(But God always heals the Brokenhearted - Psalm 147:3 - He healeth the broken in heart, and bindeth up their wounds).** It can be a loss of one's health and energy for a short season or a long season. There are many kinds of losses that cause us to walk through the valley. The valley can be a place of loneliness and darkness. Covered by clouds of gray and darkness, we may wonder if we will ever see the brightness of the sun (Son) again. We may not sense the presence of our Lord in the valley, but rest assured, He is there right beside us. Only

God knows the appointed time for each of us, as individuals, as to when we shall come out of the valley and dwell on the mountain top in the "light" again.

This again is only for a season. (**Romans 8:28 - And we know that all things work together for good to them that love God, to them who are the called according to his purpose).** When we can grasp and understand that God is always for us and with us and working His good plan out for our lives; then we can go through these times and seasons easier. (**Jeremiah 29:11 - For I know the thoughts that I think toward you, saith the LORD, thoughts of peace, and not of evil, to give you an expected end).** Also, we can have faith and encouragement knowing they will not last forever.

Another season I believe we go through, is a time of being in confusion and not being able to understand any of our circumstances. Confusion and lack of understanding is only for a season also. It's almost like we're "blind" spiritually for a season. Does God allow this? I believe so; for the purpose of teaching us to trust him more and more and ourselves and others less and less. I believe this is a season of distress. **(Psalm 4:1 - To the chief Musician on Neginoth, A Psalm of David. Hear me when I call, O God of my righteousness: thou hast enlarged me when I was in distress; have mercy upon me, and hear my prayer).** When we come out of this kind of season, I believe we gain greater insight and wisdom concerning the things of the Spirit life. God allows this to enlarge us spiritually, so we may be much more effective and fruitful in the Kingdom. **(John Chapter15)**

Another season we go through is a season of pruning. Ouch! Anyone who tends a garden or watches someone do it, learns that in order to bear better and more fruit such as grape vines or rose bushes, they must be pruned back. They appear to be almost dry and dead. But the results when they bloom again are awesome, because of greater growth and fruitfulness. God applies this principle in our spirit life also. We can feel almost dead and like we will never be fruitful and useful again, but God will cause us to be fruitful and useful in His Kingdom again, always for His glory. So if you're in this season and feel like God's done with you and will never use you again, take heart and be encouraged, this too shall pass as a season in your life.

Another season, I believe is one of affliction. **(Proverbs 24:16 - For a just man falleth seven times, and riseth up again: but the wicked shall fall into mischief).** Thank God this is only for a season. Affliction can come in many forms. It is interesting to me that we can be fruitful in the land (or time) of our affliction. (**Genesis 41:52 - And the name of the second called he Ephraim: For God hath caused me to be fruitful in the land of my affliction).** God will always be faithful and take us out of this season at just the right time, (His; not ours). We learn to trust Him more. Our faith in Him grows. We are enlarged and encouraged for the purpose of helping others to understand and to be comforted. But most of all, to bring God glory.

Another season is going through the fire. (**Malachi 3:3 - And he shall sit as a refiner and purifier of silver: and he shall purify the sons of Levi, and purge them as gold and silver, that they may offer unto the LORD an offering in righteousness).** This season purify's us and makes us holy unto God. He allows this season to burn away the dross and refine us as silver and gold. We can think we will die and not make it, if we're honest. (Sometimes we don't want to). But God's purpose for us is to be used in a greater measure and purpose. **(Isaiah 24:15 - Wherefore glorify ye the LORD in the fires, even me of the LORD God of Israel in the isles of the sea).** God is even glorified when we're in the fire. Isn't that amazing! Just look at the three Hebrews in the book of Daniel, who went into the fire; but came out not burned, and not even the smell of smoke was on them. What an awesome God we serve! The most important fact, was that the Lord was in the fire with them.

Another season is when we think we're drowning from the floods over flowing us.**(Isaiah 4:2 - When thou passest through the waters, I will be with thee; and through the rivers, they shall not overflow thee: when thou walkest through the fire, thou shalt not be burned; neither shall the flame kindle upon thee).** The floods can be any of life's circumstances that make us feel overwhelmed. They can also be the enemy of our souls coming against us. Just when we're sure we're going to drown, God reaches down and lifts us out of the water and sets us on dry, safe ground, and we see His faithfulness again.

Another season is the season of being on the Potter's wheel. **(Jeremiah 18:4 - And the vessel that he made of clay was marred in the hand of the potter: so he made it again another vessel, as seemed good to the potter to make it).** I've heard many teachings on this one, and some are often very humorous. But when we're on the potter's wheel, it doesn't seem so humorous at the time. We can be spinning around and around and cry out to God - ("Please stop, I can't take this anymore"). Guess what? You probably can and will. The Master potter knows exactly the right time to take us off the wheel and let us rest from dizziness. He may put us on the wheel again, if we're not a finished product at that time. Sorry, I know you did not want to hear that. But it's in the Word. Thank God for his love, grace, and mercy, for only He in His sovereignty knows the exact time and season of our being on the potter's wheel. Guess what? He is so faithful that He never gives up on us, even when we and others do. I don't know about you, but that's reason enough for me to continue to trust Him and praise Him and have faith in Him; because He knows exactly what He's doing. And it's always done through His love, mercy, grace, and faithfulness to us.

If you're like me, sometimes you don't want to go through all of these different seasons. [A note to Bible scholars!] I am very aware that there are probably other seasons to mention; however this book is not meant to be an in depth study of any one subject. It's only meant to touch lightly on different subjects. The reader may do an in depth study as they wish. My purpose in touching on the seasons we go through is to perhaps enlighten and especially to encourage anyone who is going through one of them. Also to proclaim that God's faithfulness is always with you which ever season you might be in. And because it's always for our good; we can learn to bear and endure these times easier and go through them more quickly.

The Heart

What kind of heart do you have? Is it hot and zealous toward the Lord, or is it cool and halfhearted? Or is it lukewarm? **(The answer is in Psalm 51: 10-12 - Create in me a pure heart, O God, and renew a steadfast spirit within me. Do not cast me from your presence or take your Holy Spirit from me. Restore to me the joy of your salvation and grant me a willing spirit, to sustain me).** Pray for a renewed and zealous heart for the Lord.

Do you have a "brokenheart"? Many things in life

can give us a brokenheart or a wounded heart. It can be from the loss of a mate, relative, friendship, or a disappointment in circumstances in our life. Many reasons cause the problem. Thank God there is a solution and answer **(Psalm 34: 18 - The LORD is close to the brokenhearted and saves those who are crushed in spirit).**

There are numerous kinds of heart conditions in the Word. Do you have a loving, joyful, peaceful heart? A heart of mercy and compassion? All these are good conditions to have and many more.

But if you have any of the less than perfect conditions of the heart, the Bible has an answer for each one. A bitter heart? An unforgiving heart? A depressed and despairing heart? A contrite and crushed heart? Isn't that interesting? We think it's a negative, but God say's it's good in his sight! **(Psalm 51:17 - The sacrifices of God are a**

broken spirit; a broken and contrite heart, O God, you will not despise).

Do you have a humble heart before the Lord, or a prideful heart? Do you have a trusting and believing heart, or a heart of doubt and unbelief? Do you have a heart of faith and wisdom? What about an unstable heart, trusting one day and not trusting the next?

With the many heart conditions in the Bible, only God can show you what kind of heart you have at any given time. (a good word study for anyone so inclined). There is an answer for every need that we may have in God's Word. God is always faithful to help and heal us when we seek Him, sincerely.

Enlargement

For anyone reading this and wondering what "enlargement" means, first it does not mean gaining weight in the natural. Wow! What a relief to know that.

It does mean having a greater capacity to love God and others, (also ourselves). Also it is for a greater capacity for patience, understanding, and wisdom. All of the fruit of the Spirit, (**Galatians 5:22-23 - But the fruit of the Spirit is love, joy, peace, longsuffering, gentleness, goodness, faith, meekness, temperance: against such there is no**

law) can be increased in us as a capacity to reach others for the Kingdom of God in a more effective way. Obvious ones are greater love and less hate and prejudice. Greater faith and less doubt and fear. Greater joy instead of sadness and mourning. Greater peace instead of unrest and turmoil in our spirit, mind, and emotions. Greater ability for self control or (temperance). A greater spirit of gentleness, kindness, and meekness. You get the picture! That's why we're a work in progress and it seems to take forever. Obviously we all have different areas of strengths and weaknesses. Maybe you have surpassed someone in one area, but they may have surpassed you in another area. That's a thought to keep one humble and less prideful! Don't you think?

Enlargement can also be God wanting to put more of His Light in us to become a greater, more effective witness to the world. He may also be wanting to give you a new gifting by His Spirit or even a new ministry.

Enlargement helps us to know and understand how the enemy comes against us so we are not stopped in our spiritual growth and so we can recognize his ways and schemes against us and others.

I wonder why it is that when we go through these times and seasons, we begin to fear, doubt, and have unbelief. We seem to forget that God has <u>always</u> been faithful to us in the past, so why not now?

Lord of All ?

This can be a tough issue for many Christians. We all want our ticket to heaven, but many of us want to live our lives in our own way, not God's. He will lead and guide us clearly if we are open and willing to be obedient. Do we want God's agendas in our lives or our own agenda? We can even think and pray for His agenda, but down deep in our hearts, we still really want our own agenda. If we are not aware of this, be assured God will show us.

We are called temples in scripture. (**1 Corinthians**

3:16 - Don't you know that you yourselves are God's temple and that God's Spirit lives in you?). If we used an illustration of ourselves as a house, does Jesus have access to <u>all</u> the rooms of our house, or do we keep certain rooms off limits to Him? Maybe even a closet with the door closed and locked, a part of our lives where we don't want Him to have access to. He will come to us again and again and ask for access to these rooms and closets in our lives, but we have the choice! (Free will). If we could only understand that He only wants the best for us, we would gladly open these doors to Him. We could save ourselves untold pain and suffering (also wasted time) if we could just let go and trust Jesus completely. He only desires to bring us healing and wholeness. (**1 Thessalonians 5:23 - May God himself, the God of peace, sanctify you through and through. May your whole spirit, soul and body be kept blameless at the**

coming of our Lord Jesus Christ).

I personally have found many times in my life that a particular physical illness or pain in my body has been healed and released after prayer for some kind of bondage or stronghold in the spirit realm affecting me. Sometimes our physical or even mental and emotional problems are simply a matter of wrong diet, lack of rest, stress, etc., in the natural realm. When these are corrected, our symptoms go away. But sometimes it is something in the spirit realm that must be dealt with. Here again, only by seeking God and asking him to show us how and what to do, is the answer. Sometimes prayer and fasting are needed. And if we cannot get a clear answer, I believe we should seek out someone who knows how to hear from God or go to a spiritual leader for help.

God is Sovereign in His providence (which we can

never comprehend; otherwise He would not be God and worthy of our trust and faith). I believe He sometimes allows an illness or pain and suffering in our bodies for a season, and for His purposes. (**Romans 8:28 - And we know that in all things God works for the good of those who love him, who have been called according to his purpose**). We can and should pray continuously for healing, but if it does not come, we can still trust Him completely. Again, He is sovereign and always in control and always knows exactly what He is doing in each one of our lives. (we may not understand completely until we get to heaven).

Remember, I told you of my mother wearing a shoe brace from polio her entire life? She often asked me why and said when she gets to heaven, she will ask the Lord why. I wonder if when we are in His wonderful, awesome and holy presence forever; if maybe those earthly problems simply won't matter anymore. Only God in His sovereignty knows the "why" of it.

I've known of many people who suffer their entire lifetime or at least for long seasons in their life. Even though we don't always understand; God's very character, being first of all faithful, can always be trusted. We cannot always trust people and circumstances, but we can always trust God completely. [Do I always trust Him and walk in victory? Unfortunately, No! Remember, I'm still a work in progress and so are you], even if you think you're already perfected. **(Philippians 1:6 - being confident of this, that he who began a good work in you will carry it on to completion until the day of Christ Jesus)**.

Allowing God to be Lord of all encompasses our families too. Do we trust Him to work out His will and purpose in their lives? What about our life mate, children, and grandchildren? One of my favorite scriptures is (**Deuteronomy 7:9 - Know therefore that the LORD your God is God; he is the faithful God, keeping his covenant of love to a thousand generations of those who love him and keep his commands**). Regardless of what I see in the lives of my loved ones, I know I can trust Him to be faithful. The key here is to understand it will be in His way and His timing, not ours. (**Isaiah 55: 8-9 - "For my thoughts are not your thoughts, neither are your ways my ways," declares the LORD. "As the heavens are higher than the earth, so are my ways higher than your ways and my thoughts than your thoughts**). Another scripture I love and and stand on is about our descendants. (**Isaiah 59:21 - "As for me, this is my covenant with them," says the LORD. "My Spirit, who is on you, and my words that I have put in your mouth will not depart from your mouth, or from

the mouths of your children, or from the mouths of their descendants). How much clearer can His word to us be! He is always faithful, not sometimes, period. The word and promises in there are the final word and bottom line. He is always faithful. You can trust Him at all times in your life and for your loved ones.

About The Author

M. Ann Billiet is one of many Christians who love the Lord and desires to obey and please Him by their lives. She has been saved and has grown as a Christian for 30 years. She and her husband, Jerry, have served the Lord in many ways; mostly in the area of intercessory prayer. She has four daughters, and four grandchildren.

She was Director of Intercessory Prayer for two years in her church. She has been a teacher of the Word in home groups for seven years. She also was part of a group who organized women's retreats for ten years.

Printed in the United States
15518LVS00002B/382-522